THE
ANCIENT ART OF
Appliqué

PATTERNS FROM THE TENTMAKERS OF CAIRO

Located in Paducah, Kentucky, the American Quilter's Society (AQS) is dedicated to promoting the accomplishments of today's quilters. Through its publications and events, AQS strives to honor today's quiltmakers and their work and to inspire future creativity and innovation in quiltmaking.

Executive Book Editor: Elaine H. Brelsford
Senior Editor: Linda Baxter Lasco
Contributing Editors: Bonnie Browning, Jenny Bowker
Graphic Design: Lynda Smith
Cover Design: Michael Buckingham
Photography: Charles R. Lynch, Bonnie Browning, Jenny Bowker

Additional copies of this book may be ordered from the American Quilter's Society, PO Box 3290, Paducah, KY 42002-3290, or online at www. AmericanQuilter.com.

Text & Artwork © 2013, American Quilter's Society
Library of Congress Cataloging-in-Publication Data

American Quilter's Society
P.O. Box 3290 • Paducah, KY 42002-3290
Fax 270-898-1173 • e-mail: orders@AQSquilt.com

Browning, Bonnie K., 1944-
  The ancient art of appliqué : patterns from the tentmakers of Cairo / by Bonnie K. Browning.
     pages cm
  Includes bibliographical references and index.
  ISBN 978-1-60460-104-6 (alkaline paper)
  1. Appliqué–Patterns. 2. Tents–Egypt–Cairo–Design and construction–Miscellanea. 3. Artisans–Egypt–Cairo–Pictorial works. I. Title.
  TT779.B764 2013
  746.44'5–dc23
                                                    2013025894

Contents

Foreword by Jenny Bowker

In 1980, I visited Egypt with my husband and children. We were living in Damascus, Syria, where my husband was a diplomat with the Australian Embassy. After seeing the pyramids and the Nile, we went for a walk—I suspect we were lost—in old Islamic Cairo.

This was not part of "tourist" Egypt. There were no souvenir touts. The quiet dignity of this place was unexpected in the hustle and bustle of Cairo. We turned onto a covered street lined with shops selling brightly colored appliqué. They adorned every wall, every door, and every surface. I remember being amazed at how far the area went, but did not buy anything. I was not a quilter then, and while it was interesting, I did not want to carry it on a long and very hot walk.

In 1991, we were living in Amman, Jordan. At the start of the first Gulf War, all Australian diplomatic families were moved to Cyprus. In the middle of that period, I took two newer children to visit Egypt. We stayed with friends and they took us to see the Street of the Tentmakers.

It was very much as I remembered it, but there were fewer tentmaker shops. I noticed many large rolls of cheap patterned fabrics, which from a distance looked like their colorful appliqué. Fast forward to 2005. I was now living

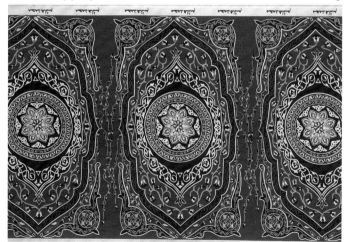

Sample of mass-produced fabric representing Khayamiya work

in Egypt. On our second day in Cairo, I returned to the Tentmakers' Street, or *Sharia Khayamiya* as the locals call it. I visited many times, sometimes several times a week. I saw brilliantly colored screens (wallhangings) in use all over Cairo in my first year.

Sometimes they were printed polyester, sometimes they were the real thing—beautiful hand-stitched appliqué. They were in the background at all sorts of celebrations: henna parties, weddings, diplomatic receptions, the locations of free meals after the fasting days during Ramadan, lining the airport when the Hajis returned from their visits to Mecca, and at funerals.

Appliqué section made for a tent

The tentmakers told me about the problems facing their profession. The cheap rolls of mass-printed fabric from China obliterated their large commissions. They sold that fabric themselves to avoid going weeks without a sale, and at least it brought some money in. But people bought that fabric instead of the tentmakers' handmade appliqué. They adapted by making smaller, finer works to hang in the homes of tourists and foreign residents. Egyptians do not buy this work—it is seen as having a connection to funerals and that is considered unlucky.

Worse, most Egyptians do not value these appliqués. There is not one piece in the Egyptian Museum or the nearby Museum of Islamic Art. Even the Egyptian Textile Museum did not have any when I was there in 2011. One Egyptian lady at a diplomatic dinner said, "Why would I want something like that 'peasant work' when I can hang a French tapestry?" Older pieces exist but they are in museums in Hawaii, or the British Museum in London, or sold on the antique market.

Old pieces can be very old indeed. In 1882, a brightly colored appliquéd tent was found in the tomb of Queen Isis em Kheb (Twenty-first Dynasty, or 900 BC). It was made of small pieces of leather in bright pink, deep golden, pale primrose, bluish green, and pale blue, with flowers on the walls and stars on the ceiling.

Tentmakers and their work are both called *Khayamiya*. In Arabic, *Khayam* means tent. Omar Khayyam's name means that someone in his family was once a tentmaker. Saint Paul was referred to as a tentmaker in the Bible.

The wonderful appliqué of today is still made on soft thick canvas, as it was when it formed the walls of a tent. They use a layer of cotton canvas as the base, a background fabric,

Mr. Mahmoud stitches in his shop.

and multiple layers of appliqué worked on top. Some people call them quilts; they just are not the three traditional layers we think of in making quilts today—a decorative top, batting or filler, and a backing held together with a running stitch that goes through all three layers. The tentmakers' work started with a different purpose—walls, not bed covers.

I was now a quilter and had travelled to many countries to work in quilt shows. One of the tentmakers told me that his family pooled their savings to send him to a furniture show in Holland, thinking he might be able to sell his appliquéd cushions. It was the wrong place for such work. He could not supply 4,000 pieces in a few weeks and for very little money like the other manufacturers. I realized that quilt shows were exactly the right place to show what these skilled men could do.

In 2007, the Australian Quilting Conference in Melbourne was happy to give us gallery space and bring two tentmakers to Australia to demonstrate their appliqué during the event. It was the first of the *Stitch Like an Egyptian* exhibitions. From there, the tentmakers' work went to France, Spain, the United Kingdom, and then to the United States. The American Quilter's Society quilt show in Grand Rapids, Michigan, was the first time that either of our stitchers, Hosam Hanafy and Tarek Abdelhay, had been to the United States, and the first time that an exhibition of Egyptian tentmaker work had been shown here.

The American Quilter's Society has given a solid promise of future work for these men. Many stitchers who left the street to work elsewhere are now starting to return. The Egyptian Revolution of January 2011 saw the end of tourism as they knew it. It might have closed their businesses, but regular international exhibitions have helped them to survive. Their work is now finer and smaller than it used to be, in order to appeal to those who wish to display it inside their homes.

I am proud to be associated with a group of such wonderful artists, and with such kind, talented, hardworking, affectionate, and gentle men. They are truly ambassadors for their country, and their appliqué work is truly unique.

Jenny Bowker, Hosam Hanafy, and Tarek Abdelhay at AQS QuiltWeek™ – Grand Rapids, Michigan 2012.

The Tentmakers of Cairo

Then and Now

The tentmakers have passed their stitching technique from father to son for generations. Today, many of the shops in Cairo are run by the second-, third-, and even fourth-generation tentmakers. Since the Revolution of 2011 and loss of the tourist trade, many stitchers have sought other work.

As far back as 900 AD, the city of Cairo was a walled city. Across from one of the original gates in that wall is the Street of the Tentmakers. It's one of the only areas in Cairo where there's still a roof over the street.

Vehicles, carts pulled by animals, and people all traverse the street.

There are tiny tentmaker shops up and down the street, but fewer now than in the past. Tentmaker work has been done since 1100 BC but the tentmakers themselves are considered on the same level as street laborers. Their work is not valued within Egypt as it is elsewhere.

In earlier times, the shops extended much farther—even beyond the covered area of the street. But the number of tentmakers went from about 479 to 250 in the period between 1979 and 1991. Over the years, the demand for the handwork has been satisfied by cheap, rip-stop fabrics printed with tentmaker designs. Today, there are only about 55 tentmakers stitching their appliquéd designs.

However, with new outlets for and interest in their work outside of Egypt, stitchers are coming back to do the tentmaking work. There was a ten percent increase in their number in just one recent three-month period. Through Jenny Bowker's efforts in taking the tentmakers' work to other countries, new frontiers have opened where the appliqué artistry of these talented stitchers is appreciated.

Young stitchers have returned to the shops to stitch. Mohamed Gamal, from Essam Ali's shop, sits on the bench whipping his long needle through the fabric to tack it to the background. Watching him manipulate those large scissors to cut and clip is like seeing a maestro wield his baton to create beautiful music.

Mohamed Gamal, even though he is young, handles his needle like a pro.

The Origin of Tentmaking

Screens or hangings are called tentmaker work because originally they were used as the walls of tents. The plain canvas backing formed the outside walls of the tents and the appliqué work decorated the inside. It was specifically designed to awe and inspire visitors. With the sun on the walls, the appliqué looked like stained glass.

In addition, the pieces are hung at every kind of celebration, from pre-wedding street gatherings to wakes and funerals.

Henna parties are held the night before a wedding. Henna is applied to the bridal party and there is dancing in the streets which are hung with tentmaker screens.

Today, screens and tents are set up to create areas for people to sit during wakes—celebrations of life—with chairs lined up for the mourners.

Interestingly, there is no differentiation between the designs used for weddings and street celebrations and those used for funerals.

The screens (or wallhangings) are all hand appliquéd and are approximately 6 yards high and 3½ – 4 yards wide. They are meant for street work and to be seen from a distance, not for close-up inspection. The visual impact of the design and color is the important thing, so the stitches are large and all done with the same thread, not matched to the fabrics.

Tentmakers of Today

Today, the tentmakers are the designers and expert stitchers who run a shop or gallery with a stable of stitchers who are given specific designs to do. The stitchers are sometimes allowed to choose their own colors to complete the work. The large pieces are not as popular with the stitchers unless they're commissioned and partially paid up front.

Only one man works on a screen, regardless of its size, so there is no dispute about who did the most work. The exception would be when a shop owner assists one of his stitchers on a large piece. A queen-size piece can take about four months to complete. The stitching is done quickly with big stitches. The more quickly the piece is finished, the sooner the tentmaker can be paid. There's a saying: "A slow stitcher has a hungry family."

The appliqué is done with commercially available fabric that is softer than quilters typically use. It rolls under easily and is stitched according to a pattern drawn on a background fabric that is laid over canvas.

Amr El Naem and Hosni Mohamed Hosni stitch in a workroom with their supplies spread out around them.

Bolts of fabric used by the tentmakers

The canvas acts something like an under-thimble quilters would use. They bounce the needle off the canvas, picking up just a few threads of the canvas as they stitch. The tentmakers cut their threads two- to three-feet long but amazingly, it doesn't tangle. They work so quickly that in photos taken of them at work, their arms are blurred.

It is hard to take a good photo of the men stitching; they stitch so quickly that the picture is usually blurry.

The shops are small—only two to three yards wide. The finished work is doubled and folded over onto itself and stacked up so that all the colors they have are visible to potential buyers. Older men are positioned out in front to chat with visitors. The real work goes on in the rooms away from the shops. The walls are always painted white to get the maximum light from the strip fluorescent bulbs. The men sit on the floor and lean against the wall as they work.

Mustapha Hasham stitches a beautiful piece of artwork.

There are some women stitchers, almost exclusively relatives or wives of the tentmakers, who have been taught to stitch by their brothers or husbands.

Eight-fold design with lotus by Wafa, a female stitcher

The Tentmakers' Technique

To make a pattern, they start with a piece of paper as large as the entire design. They fold it in half, forming a rectangle; in half again, forming a square; then in half again to form a triangle—much like we fold paper to make snowflakes. They draw one-eighth of the design on the paper, then use a needle embedded in a cork or tied to a pencil to make holes along the lines to transfer the design to all the layers of the paper pattern.

They unfold and lay the paper over the background fabric and sprinkle charcoal or cinnamon (if a light fabric) or talc or baby powder (if a dark fabric) over the paper and rub it through, making tiny dots on the fabric. Finally, they draw along the dots with a lead or white pencil, completing the transfer of the design. Only the background is marked, not the pieces to be appliquéd. This same technique has been used for the past 4000 years.

The Ancient Art of Appliqué

Sayed Aziz Shop. Lotus design from an eight-fold pattern.

Sometimes they will fold the paper one more time and draw one-sixteenth of the design.

Um Aber/Kamal and Sons Shop. Romy and lotus in sixteen-fold design with concentric rings.

Design Sources

The tentmakers find inspiration all around themselves, from geometric carvings in wood or bronze on Islamic doors to the much more fluid designs based on calligraphy.

Tarek Fattoh Shop. Islamic Mosque door design.

They use a variety of different design styles in their Khayamiya artwork. Some of the shops may stitch mainly Islamic appliqué, while others combine Romy with some Islamic appliqué to make their own unique designs.

Al Farouk Shop. Medhat combined an Eight-Pointed Elongated Star with Romy and lotus.

Some designs are reminiscent of Celtic appliqué, winding over and under, but are undoubtedly Islamic in origin. They are based on the ceilings of mosques, floors, or wall tile designs. The patterns for these are folded in squares (four-layer patterns) rather than triangles (eight- to sixteen-layer patterns).

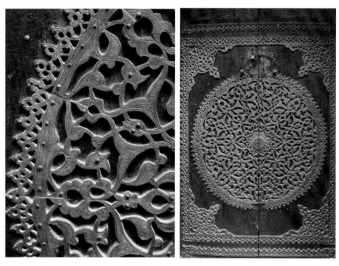

El Usefy Mosque is a good example of the Romy design.

Hossam Hashem Shop. Traditional Islamic design, 98" x 98".

Romy appliqué incorporates a distinctive little curlicue that comes from the era of the Fatimids. At this time, the calligraphy permitted in mosques was embellished with small curls and tips that looked like growing plants or leaflets.

Romy is always appliquéd with the line on top and a different colored background. It often, like Celtic work, winds over and under, but is not restrained by the same rules as Celtic work. Romy is allowed two "overs" or two "unders."

The door to the El Usefy Mosque in Old Cairo is a good example of how the design goes over and under.

Mohamed Dendon Shop. Complex Romy design, 47" x 47", by Mohamed Dendon.

Islamic appliqué is not so different from Romy, but more restrained in color and design. Islamic appliqué is usually appliquéd so that the winding line is actually the background. This allows long narrow points that would not be possible otherwise. It tends to be more traditional in design and color—gold, dark red, navy, cream, and smoky blues.

The Ancient Art of Appliqué

Khaled Mohe El Den Shop. Traditional Islamic design by Mohamed Suleiman.

There are *folkloric designs* such as the folk tale of Goha and the donkey, the wise fool, and the typical village scenes.

Hosam/Al Farouk Shop. Goha and the Donkey stitched by Mohtaz, 39" x 41". The story is read from right to left. The lesson of the story is that you can never please everyone!

The ancient art of calligraphy is not ignored and allows the master craftsmen of the street to stitch beautiful calligraphic works of art from the Koran, as well as expand their imaginations by creating animals and birds out of words and sayings.

Ashraf Hashem Shop. Calligraphy Boat by Ashraf Hashem.

Calligraphy designs can never be turned into a cushion because the text is usually from the Koran and it would be disrespectful to sit on it.

Paintings from the tombs inspire very different designs. The Nile or water is always shown as a vertical zigzag. Trees represent the tree of life with birds. A single hoopoe bird is always facing left—toward the side of the Nile where the tombs are. It is considered bad luck if one lands in your garden. It means there will be a death. The other birds face the side of the Nile where the sun rises, signifying life. Bird pieces cost more because of the extra embroidery work they entail.

Ali/Amr Hassan Sheik Shop. Hoopoe and the tree of life; east/west; life/death; 36" x 36".

One of the most common motifs is the lotus flower, though wild lotus is rare in the Nile now. When drawing the lotus, the point or the center of the lotus flower may be positioned at the paper pattern folds, or the full design may be drawn.

Tarek Fattoh Shop. Simple lotus design, 39" x 51".

Other pieces show scenes from village life. It's acceptable to include people as long as it is for a secular purpose, but they may not be shown in a mosque. Often people are depicted without facial features.

Scene featuring musicians by Mohamed Farag

Pharaonic pieces are usually done as souvenir pieces for tourists with designs resembling those from the tombs or palaces of ancient times combined with motifs from nature.

The pharaonic pieces often tell a story, like the feather and heart story of this piece.

The feather was shown in scenes of the Hall of Ma'at. This hall is where the deceased was judged for his worthiness to enter the afterlife. The seat of the deceased's soul, his heart, was weighed on a balance against the feather of Ma'at. If the heart was free from the impurities of sin, and therefore lighter than the feather, then the dead person could enter the eternal afterlife.

Those with a one-way orientation are used as prayer mats. They are copies of the niches in mosques. They are hung on the walls in homes and are used to indicate the direction of Mecca, which is the direction faced when praying.

Tarek Fattoh Shop. Mihrab design based on the curved niche in a mosque.

The Ancient Art of Appliqué

Some of these patterns are incredibly difficult to draft, yet are masterfully executed by the tentmakers in their appliqué. There are 12-Pointed Stars, 13-Pointed Stars, 24-Pointed Stars, and even 25-Pointed Stars. They are all appliquéd—none of the design is pieced.

New Opportunities

The tentmakers' work was first shown outside of Egypt at an exhibit in Australia.

Ahmed Naguib accompanied the exhibit and demonstrated the tentmakers' technique during the show. When he arrived in Australia, he knew no English. By the time he returned home, he had learned five words and phrases from hearing them repeated over and over: "amazing," "incredible," "unbelievable, isn't it?" and "look at it!"

The enthusiastic response to the exhibit totally changed the way the men perceived their own work. They all started to walk with their heads held higher. People were in tears as they listened to Ahmed talk about the response to his work.

"They CLAPPED when I finished one flower. I will never again listen to [someone] who is trying to tell me my work is rubbish, that my prices should be half or that he will only pay half of what he agreed to in the beginning. I will never believe it again because in Australia they clapped for one flower!"

Michelle Hill does appliqué based on William Morris's work and Ahmed Naguib was inspired to copy a piece of hers that he saw in a catalog. He wanted to take the piece to Australia, but Jenny told him he couldn't since it was a copy of someone else's work. But he still wanted to include it in the exhibit.

Jenny asked, "What would happen if the man in the next shop copied your work?"

"We would have to fight," Ahmed responded.

"Well, Michelle might fight you."

"Is she big?"

Michelle was so charmed when she heard this story, she gave him access to all her patterns. He, in turn, sent the piece to her.

William Morris-inspired piece stitched by Ahmed Naguib, designed by Michelle Hill

Mohamed Sheban, another tentmaker, visited France in 2007 with an exhibit.

Mohamed Sheban visits with quilters in France.

Jenny thought he might be uncomfortable sitting in a Catholic church, but he said, "My religion isn't in a building, it's in here," as he tapped his chest over his heart.

An exhibition was hung in a gallery in Aracena, Spain, in 2008. This was the first time any of the tentmakers had seen their work in such a setting. Suddenly, they could see and appreciate their work as fine art. Coincidentally, tiles outside the gallery in Spain had the same pattern as the appliqué work done in Egypt.

Tiles on buildings in Spain are very similar to designs used by the tentmakers in Egypt.

Tentmaker Hossam Hashem has secured a contract to provide bedspreads for the beds in boutique Talisman Hotels in Cairo and Damascus, convincing the owners that they can get more for their rooms if he decorates them. The rooms are painted bright colors and he makes the spreads to coordinate with them. Matching narrow borders are made for the plain linen curtains.

Other tentmakers are stitching pieces based on an artist's work, offering to translate their work in other media to the tentmaker canvas. Algerian artist Rachid Koraïchi commissioned ninety-nine pieces to be exhibited at the Islamic museum in Paris. He sent his designs

on transparencies. They were enlarged, transferred, and stitched by the tentmakers.

Commissioned piece based on the artwork of Rachid Koraïchi

The commission had to be done within a year. It might have been impossible, but by hiring additional stitchers, the commission was completed. This is just a portion of the finished pieces ready for shipping.

Some of the pieces commissioned by artist Rachid Koraïchi are ready for shipment.

The Ancient Art of Appliqué

Appliqué Designs from the Tentmakers' Shops

Preparing the Pattern

The tentmakers often use designs that can be made by folding paper to create a pattern, similar to the way we make snowflakes or the way Hawaiian quiltmakers would make a quilt pattern. Usually the pattern is ⅛ of the whole design.

- Use a piece of paper that is at least 2" larger than your finished design; that is, 1" extra on all four sides.

- Fold the paper in half and crease along the fold.

- Open the paper and fold in half in the opposite direction; crease along the fold. Open.

- Fold the paper in half from corner to corner on the diagonal; crease along the fold. Open.

- Fold the paper in half from the opposite corners on the diagonal; crease along the fold.

- You will now have the paper folded in eighths. Open the paper and lay the paper on the pattern, matching the corners. Trace the design on one-eighth of the paper.

- Fold the paper so only the eighth of the design with the pattern drawn on it shows.

- Put three or four staples in areas where there are no lines to hold the paper together securely.

- Using a large needle or an awl, punch holes through all layers of the paper; or you can put a #90 or #100 needle in your sewing machine—no thread is needed. You will be perforating the paper with the needle.

- Stitch over every line on the pattern to punch holes in the pattern.

Design for ⅛ of a pattern

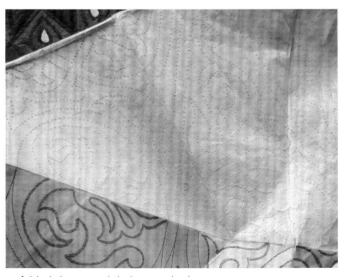

Unfolded design with holes punched

Transferring the Pattern to the Background Fabric

- Cut the background fabric at least 2" larger than the desired finished size.

- Remove the staples from the pattern.

- Open the pattern and center it on the background.

- Using baby powder on dark fabric or cinnamon on light fabric, rub or pounce the powder over the holes in the pattern.

- Carefully pull away the paper.

- Trace over all of the dotted lines with a pencil; use a white pencil for dark backgrounds or a mechanical pencil for light backgrounds.

- Shaking the background fabric should remove most of the powder, which is no longer needed after you have marked over the design with a pencil.

Appliquéing the Design

Use your favorite appliqué method for stitching the design.

The tentmakers use a technique that is very different from the techniques today's quilters use. They simply lay down a piece of fabric and trim it as they stitch, carefully following the design marked on the background. In some cases, they may lay a piece the same size as the background down and trim as they go to stitch some of the elements in place if that particular color is used throughout the piece. For multiple colors, they will then select a piece for the next layer of color for their design.

The following photos show how they add layer after layer.

Pieces are cut and appliquéd in place as you go.

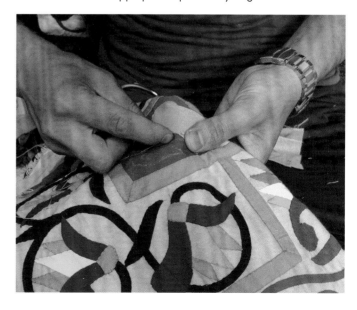

The Ancient Art of Appliqué

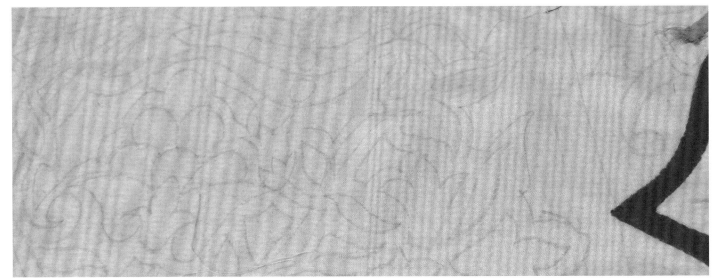

Pattern marked on the background.

Designs are marked on the background fabric, with multiple layers of appliqué.

The hand in the photo shows the scale of the designs being applied.

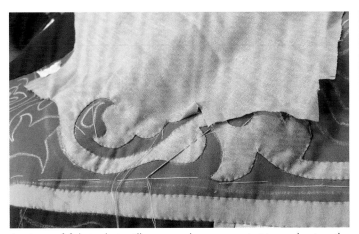

A piece of fabric that will cover a large area is trimmed using the design marked on the background fabric as a guide.

Yahya trims the fabric as he stitches.

Cushions from the Tentmakers of Cairo

Eighteen shops contributed designs to make pillow covers.
Each of the designs finish to 14" x 14". Add borders to make the cushion
cover the desired size, or stitch several designs to make an entire quilt.

Use the designs that follow to make your own piece of Egyptian Khayamiya art.

The Ancient Art of Appliqué

احمد عاطف

Ahmed Atef Fattoh

The Ancient Art of Appliqué   22

©Ahmed Atef Fattoh 2013

The Ancient Art of Appliqué

احمد عاطف

Ahmed Atef Fattoh/Hany Fattoh Shop

The Ancient Art of Appliqué

The Ancient Art of Appliqué

Ahmed Goma

The Ancient Art of Appliqué 26

©Ahmed Goma 2013

27

The Ancient Art of Appliqué

أحمد لبيب عادل

Ahmed Naguib

The Ancient Art of Appliqué   28

©Ahmed Naguib 2013

The Ancient Art of Appliqué

Ahmed Rora

The Ancient Art of Appliqué

Amr Hashem Sheik

The Ancient Art of Appliqué

©Amr Hashem Sheik 2013

The Ancient Art of Appliqué

Ashraf Hashem

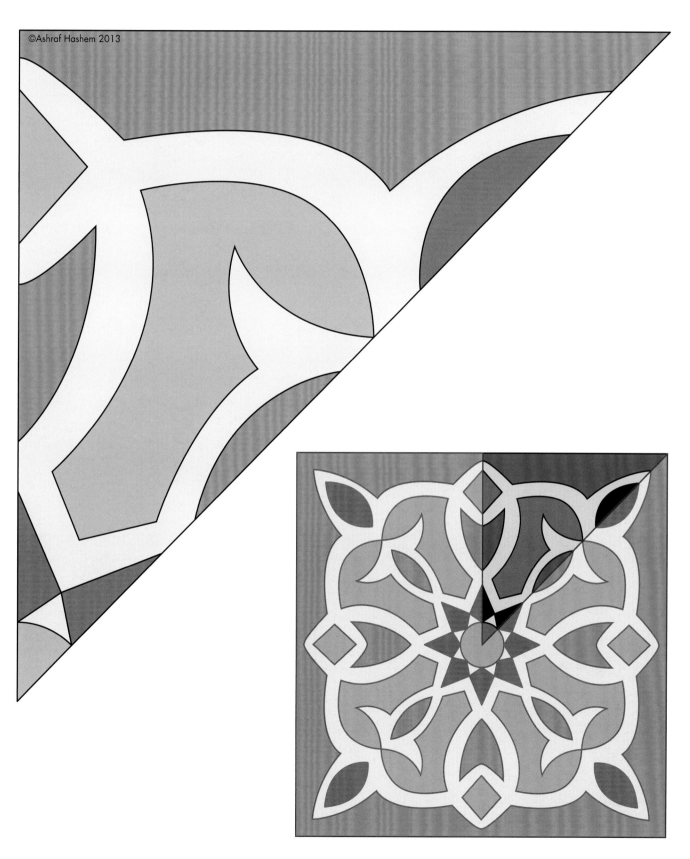

©Ashraf Hashem 2013

35   The Ancient Art of Appliqué

Essem Ali

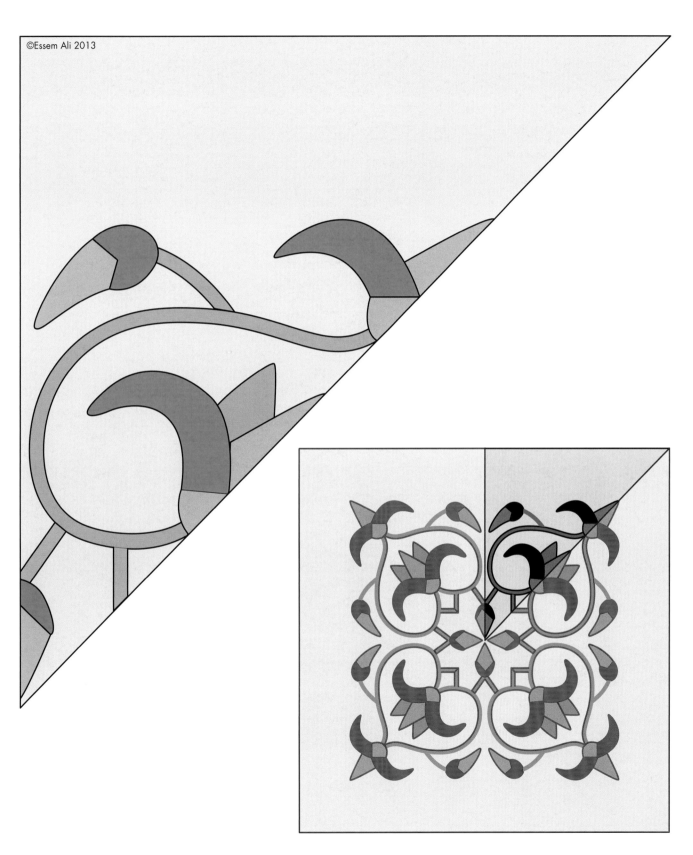

37   The Ancient Art of Appliqué

فوز

Fauzy Nounou

The Ancient Art of Appliqué   38

The Ancient Art of Appliqué

Gamal Kalthouma

The Ancient Art of Appliqué   40

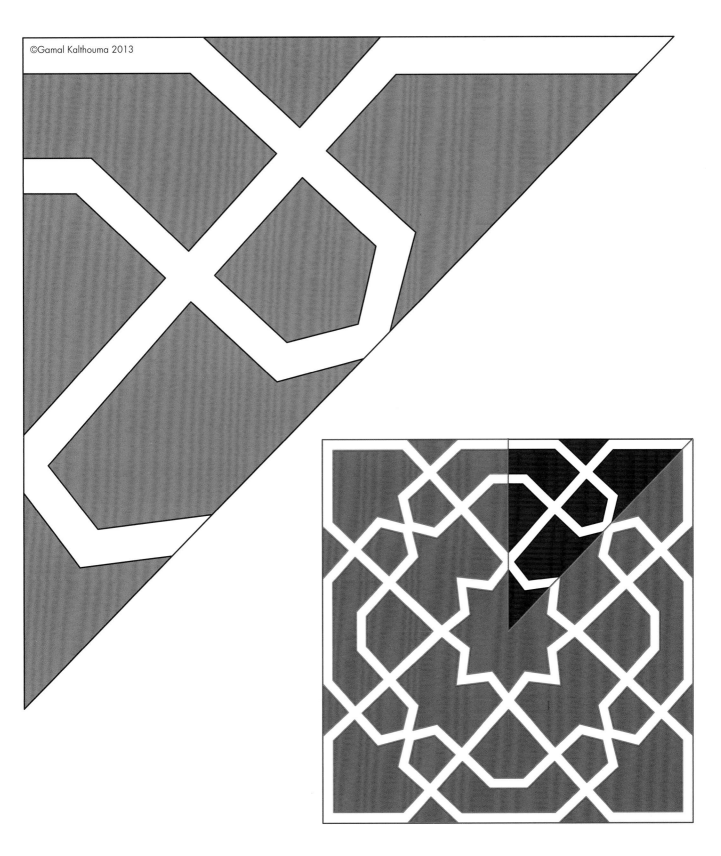

©Gamal Kalthouma 2013

The Ancient Art of Appliqué

Hassan Kamal

©Hassan Kamal 2013

Place on fold

Connect to design on page 44

The Ancient Art of Appliqué

Connect to design on page 43

©Hassan Kamal 2013

Place on fold

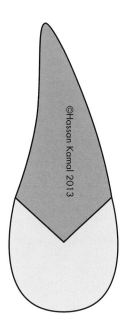

©Hassan Kamal 2013

The Ancient Art of Appliqué

Hosam Hanafy/Al Farouk Shop

The Ancient Art of Appliqué

©Al Farouk Shop 2013

The Ancient Art of Appliqué

Khaled Mohe El Den

©Khaled Mohe El Den 2013

The Ancient Art of Appliqué

Mohamed Dendon

©Mohamed Dendon 2013

The Ancient Art of Appliqué

Mohamed Ibrahim

©Mohamed Ibrahim 2013

The Ancient Art of Appliqué

Mohamed Morsi

©Mohamed Morsi 2013

The Ancient Art of Appliqué

Ramy Hashem/Mohamed Hashem Shop

The Ancient Art of Appliqué

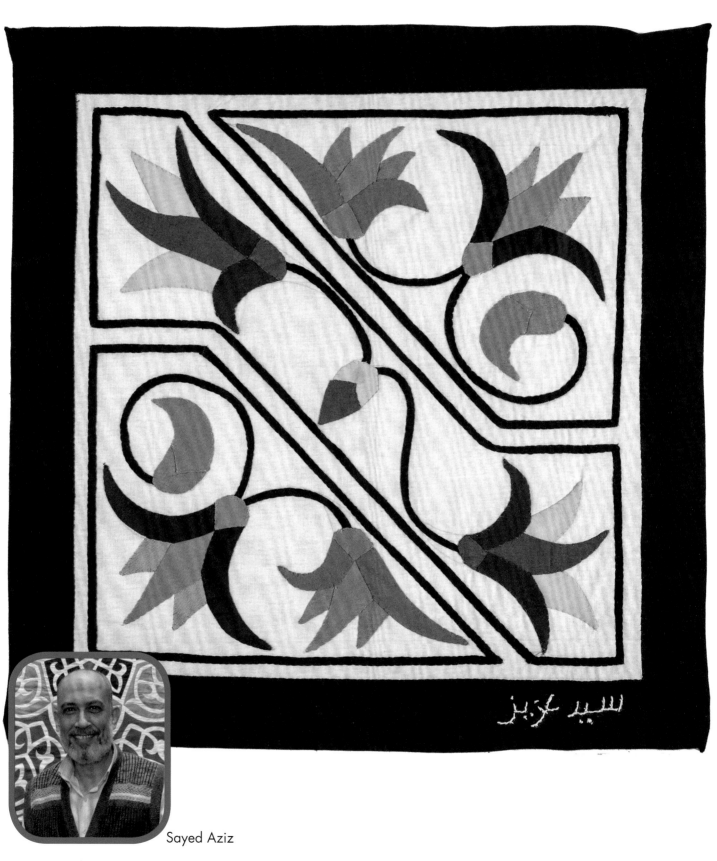

Sayed Aziz

©Sayed Aziz 2013

59

©Sayed Aziz 2013

Place on fold

©Sayed Aziz 2013

The Ancient Art of Appliqué

Meet Bonnie Browning

Bonnie has been sewing since her mother taught her to sew on a treadle sewing machine as a child. Creating the annual family Christmas ornament led to making clothing and finally quilts. She made her first quilt top in 1979; it was a sampler that has never been quilted but it was a great learning tool.

Bonnie has won numerous awards with her quilting. Two of her quilts, A LITTLE BIT OF CANDLEWICKING and SMITTEN WITH FLOWERS, are in the collection of The National Quilt Museum located in Paducah, Kentucky. Two of her quilts are in the Artists of Iowa Collection in her home state of Iowa.

Bonnie has been the executive show director for the American Quilter's Society since 1994. She is a professional quilt instructor, a certified quilt judge, and a Certified Zentangle Teacher. Bonnie has traveled around the world teaching in Australia, Canada, Indonesia, Japan, and Turkey; quilting has also taken her to the Bernina Teachers Reunion in Switzerland. Bonnie has written eleven books on quilting, published by the American Quilter's Society. She finds quilting is a universal language and quilters can easily communicate with fabric, needles, and thread.

Having the opportunity to visit Cairo, Egypt, in 2012 and 2013 to select some of the tentmakers' appliqué art for AQS exhibitions added another first. Seeing the pyramids and ancient tombs first-hand, getting to know the tentmakers on their home land, and sailing on the Nile River are all memorable parts of those visits. It is easy to appreciate the talent of the tentmakers: their use of color; the dexterity and speed with which they wield their needles; and how they manage to make such precise cuts with their scissors, which are huge in our eyes.

Working on this book has given Bonnie another means to share the tentmakers' work with quilters around the world, and to give quilters a chance to make their own piece of Khayamiya.

Meet Jenny Bowker

Jenny Bowker has been working in textiles since 1997, from the time she finished a bachelor of arts degree in the visual arts and decided to make just one quilt.

Her life before quilting was in science. Now she is moving toward melding her fine art work with her textile work. She is interested in the way pattern comes into so many parts of our lives. She often includes some geometrical piecing in her work as she thinks it keeps her technically on her toes and provides a key for traditional quilters to connect to her work.

Jenny has four children and a very supportive husband who worked as a diplomat for the Department of Foreign Affairs and Trade. While following him, she lived a total of fifteen years in Arab and Islamic countries: Syria, Western Samoa, Malaysia, Jordan, Jerusalem, and Egypt. This might seem irrelevant to quilting, but it has influenced her subject matter and much of Jenny's work reflects her love of the Middle East.

She enjoys teaching and has done so around the world. "There is no greater delight than to offer tools to quilters who want to make original work but don't know how to access their own ideas."

In addition to teaching, Jenny's work has been exhibited from Africa to the United States and many points in between.

Jenny was curator of the first *Stitch Like an Egyptian* exhibition of the tentmakers' work held in Australia in 2006. Since that time, she has curated other exhibits of their work in France, Spain, England, and the United States. With first-hand knowledge gained from her time in the Middle East, Jenny's lectures make the tentmakers and their work come alive.

Photo by Sam Bowker

The Ancient Art of Appliqué

more AQS books

This is only a small selection of the books available from the American Quilter's Society. AQS books are known worldwide for timely topics, clear writing, beautiful color photos, and accurate illustrations and patterns. The following books are available from your local bookseller, quilt shop, or public library.

#8932

#8529

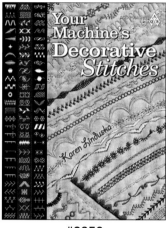

#8353

#8532

#8664

#1423

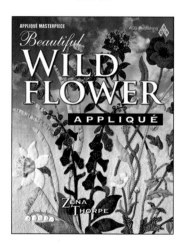

#8526

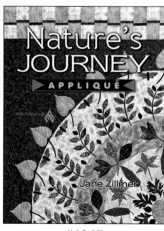

#1247

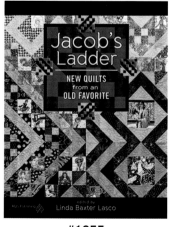

#1255

LOOK for these books nationally.
CALL or **VISIT** our website at

1-800-626-5420
www.AmericanQuilter.com